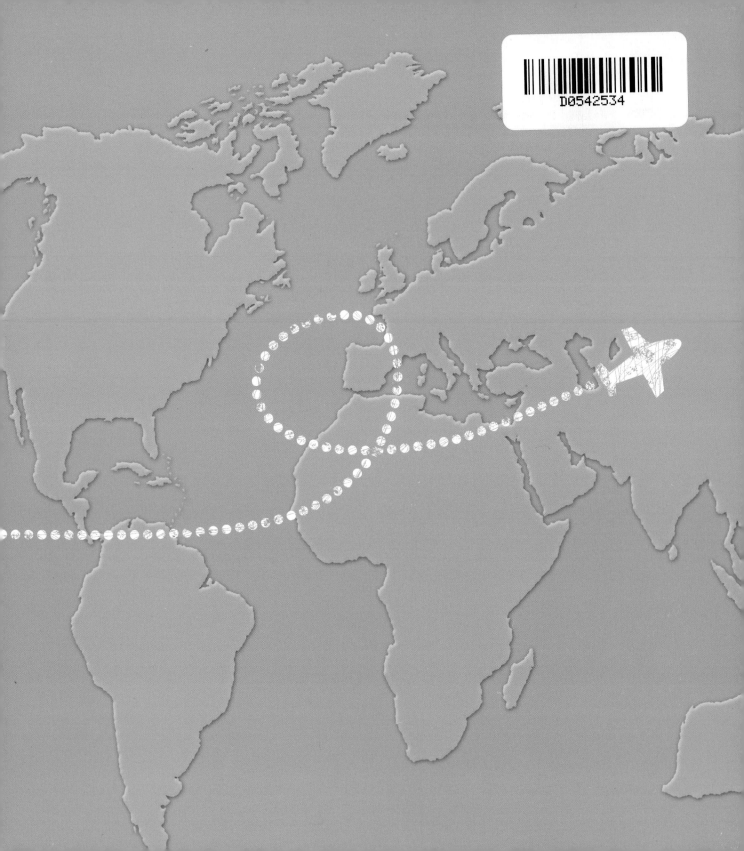

This book belongs to:

EGMONT

We bring stories to life

First published in Great Britain in 2006
by Egmont UK Limited
239 Kensington High Street, London W8 6SA
Illustrated by Artful Doodlers and Niall Harding
Postman Pat © 2006 Woodland Animations Ltd,
a division of Entertainment Rights PLC.
Licensed by Entertainment Rights PLC.
Original writer John Cunliffe.
From the original television design by Ivor Wood
Royal Mail and Post Office imagery is used by kind
permission of Royal Mail Group plc.
All rights reserved.

ISBN 978 1 4052 2411 6
ISBN 1 4052 2411 8
1 2 3 4 5 6 7 8 9 10
Printed in China

Holiday Fun with Postman Pat ®

Jeff and Charlie Pringle are on holiday in Paris, France. They're riding all over the city on bikes.

"Next stop the Eiffel Tower!" shouts Jeff. "Hang on to your beret, Charlie!"

"I can't wait to climb up to the top," says Charlie. "It used to be the tallest building in the world!"

Charlie's favourite facts about France:

One day, I think I'll enter the Tour de France and race through the French countryside on my bike!

Dad tried lots of smelly cheese!

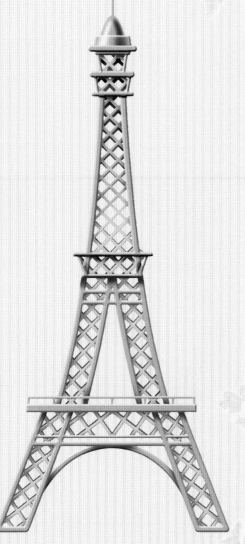

Dad and I climbed up the Eiffel Tower. It took us ages!

Find France on the map and add the sticker of Charlie

Postman Pat is on holiday in Australia with Sara and Julian. Today, they've been snorkelling in the Great Barrier Reef.

"I saw a turtle," says Julian, "and a shark!"

"A shark?!" says Pat, turning white.

"Don't worry, Dad, it was only a little one," says Julian.

Julian's favourite facts about Australia:

Snakes swallow their prey whole!

I was scared of all the snakes and spiders!

Ayers Rock

Ayers Rock is the second **biggest** rock in the world!

We saw a kangaroo. It had a baby in a pouch on its tummy!

Find Australia on the map and add the sticker of Julian

PC Selby and Lucy are on holiday in Egypt. Today, they're visiting the Great Pyramid.

"The ancient kings of Egypt were buried in pyramids," says PC Selby. "They used to be full of treasure, but now it has all been stolen!"

"That wouldn't have happened if you'd been there, Dad," says Lucy, proudly

Lucy's favourite facts about Egypt:

by LUCY

If I were an
Egyptian Queen,
I would be like
Cleopatra!

Even Dad couldn't read the
funny Egyptian writing!

When a King died in ancient
Egypt, he was wrapped in
lots of bandages. And
then he was called
a mummy!

Find Egypt on the map
and add the sticker of Lucy

The Pottage family are in Florida in America. Today, they're at a theme park. The twins have been on a ferris wheel, a roller-coaster and a very wet water ride. But now, Mrs Pottage seems to have lost them!

"Are you looking for these two?" asks a tall clown with Tom and Katy on his shoulders.

Tom and Katy's favourite facts about America:

Rockets zoom into space from a launch pad at Cape Canaveral in Florida.

We swam with the dolphins. They can do roly polys in the air!

Scary crocodiles live in a swampy place called the Everglades!

Find America on the map and add the sticker of Tom

Ajay Bains is on holiday in India with Nisha, Meera and Nikhil.
Today, they're visiting the Taj Mahal.

"An emperor built the Taj Mahal for his beloved wife," says Nisha,
dreamily. "I think it's the most beautiful building in the world."

"Are there any trains near here?" wonders Ajay, out loud.

Meera and Nikhil's favourite facts about India:

Taken by Ajay

Over a million people work for the Indian railway system.

(This is dad's favourite fact!)

There are lots of tigers in India. Every tiger has a different pattern of stripes on its fur!

Meera

We saw an elephant squirting water with its long trunk!!

Find India on the map and add the sticker of Meera

Dr Gilbertson and Sarah are in Kenya on an African safari. They're travelling everywhere in a Jeep.

"Look at those stripy ponies," says Sarah, pointing. "They don't look much like Snowbella."

"Those are zebras," says Dr Gilbertson, "and, no, you can't ride them!"

Sarah's favourite facts about Kenya:

A giraffe is the tallest animal in the world. Look at its really long neck!

Our Jeep has really strong tyres so that it can speed over rocks!

Sarah

Leopards carry their food up a tree so that no other animal can eat it!

Find Kenya on the map and add the sticker of Sarah

Mrs Goggin's favourite animal facts from around the world:

I love hearing the children's favourite world facts. Here are some of my favourite animal facts - and a few questions!

The elephant lives in Africa and Asia. It has a long nose called a trunk. What does it like to do with it?

The giant panda lives in China. It has five fingers and one thumb.

The kangaroo lives in Australia. What special thing does it keep in its pouch?

The parrot lives in warm countries like South America. It can repeat what you say to it!

It can repeat what you say to it!

The lion lives in Africa. It is part of the cat family and can sleep for as many as 20 hours a day! Which other famous Greendale resident is part of the cat family?

ZZZzz

The penguin lives in cold snowy places. The largest penguin is the Emperor Penguin which grows 3ft 7in tall!

Can you find the pictures of the panda, penguin, parrot and lion on the map?

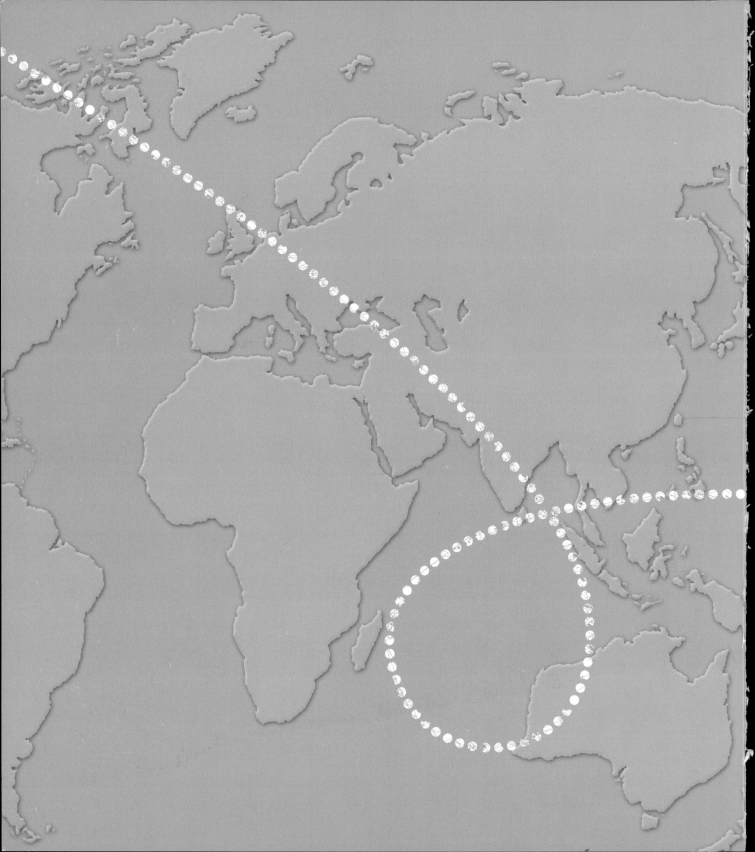